WHEN PETALS FALL

An Anthology of Poetry

WHEN PETALS FALL

An Anthology of Poetry

Kate Brumby
Ebom Tobe Churchill
Simphiwe Sihawu Dlamini
Simran Munot
Brian Ngusale
Surendra Sahu
Venessa Valdez

DEDICATIONS

My poems were written following the tragic and unexpected death of Stuart Richard Allister aged 56 years on May 18th, 2019. They are dedicated to Stu and his wife and soul mate, my cousin, Sally Allister. I hope I have done them both proud.

My share of royalties will be donated to www.lionrescue.org.za, where a young lion has been named in memorial of Stu.

-Kate Brumby-

For Ndidi

I didn't know I was in love
With the morning mist
And the sun comes out too early
In West Africa
And just like that she faded
Like she never happened
I'm left alone, biting my thoughts
To stir up memories
No matter what I say
I cannot sugar-coat my grief
Grief is grief, nothing more
And nothing can be done
To change it.

-Ebom Tobe Churchill-

For my late father who passed when I was three

-Simphiwe Sihawu Dlamini-

I would like to dedicate *When Petals Fall* to anyone who has or is enduring pain, suffered an addiction, felt powerless or has or may be walking in the darkness of depression.

Please know, you are not in this fight alone.
There is light inside of you.

For those that stood by my side through my darkest hours and continue to, no matter how rough the sailing may become. I wouldn't be alive if it wasn't for you.

Jim Valdez(dad): My life support
Robert Damron: My heart
Evelynn Damron: My soul
Denise Palmer: My rock
Stevi Laduna: The compassionate one
Joni Phillips: The brutally honest one
Roger Palmer: The tolerant one

A Message to my Daughter:

May you never have to walk the dark roads I have.
I love you always and forever
Love, Mommy

-Venessa Valdez-

CONTENTS

INTRODUCTION

Whether you enter from a place of emptiness, loss, grief, despair or recovery, these pages offer understanding, compassion and console. We welcome you to explore the multi-facets of the raw emotion of sadness through which the words on the pages paint distinct pictures.

Fewer than three months since the germination of the idea of bringing together poetry from diverse cultures around the globe; *When Petals Fall* blossomed. Comprised of seven 'down to earth' poets from across four continents; Africa, Asia, Europe and North America. With poetry styles as diverse as the poets who have written them, each poem offers an opportunity to resonate wherever you are in the world.

Written presumably across dissimilar places and times; *When Petals Fall* stands out as an ornament and a timeless pearl to lovers of poetry all over the world. Offering an escape to dip in and out of or return to time and time again. A book that is beyond words.

Cor ad cor loquitor!

Our hearts speak to yours!

You are not alone

Gone Too Soon

Memories cry out like lost children
As I pretend they don't exist
My peace is compromised
Despair is now a hymn
I'm the only chorister.

A day doesn't end without a song
The hours don't repeat themselves
Without a scream of sorrow
You are tenderer than cattle-birds
That love it best in waters
My tears will make you a river
If you will swim back.

Nne, the blooms are up again
The rains have started
The playground is filled up
And there you lay, wrapped up
There you lay, wasting away
In the dust.

You keep calling me from your ruins
Cold dead face, sand-coated eyes
You keep calling me
As tired sunset calls the night

You keep calling me

And you will keep calling

Because you can't hear my voice

You don't know I'm crying out

Raising my weathered head

To the cold sun.

Someone should comfort me with a lie

I want to hear that you are not dead

Can snow decompose?

Don't tell me it melts away

Please, by the gods, please.

I am decaying

But I won't complain

You decayed first

You never complained

I will tell you about an endless night

Buried in the womb of pains and mourning

I am that frosty midnight.

Why will I cry all day?

When you aren't far away

I'll swallow up my biggest fear

And scold you when I meet you there.

I've been walking all alone

Drifting to a place unknown

Hoping to fall and turn dry bone

So I can forget you at last

Because you buried me

Just to stay away from me

You won't do so never again.

My tears have made so much salt

That it seems Lot's wife slept here

You would've smiled your smile

You would've looked me in the eye

Like a psychologist

You said you wouldn't leave

I thought there was a rainbow

I thought there was hope

But I was wrong

Just like you.

When I think of flowers

Freckled in dew

I remember you

You are not the flower

You are the dew

Gone too soon.

Ebom Tobe Churchill

Forgiven, Not Forgotten

Banished into the sea of forgetfulness
Where man nor angels tread
The hurts and remorse of the past
Were deposited before she fled.

With quickness of movement there
She was eager to release emotion
And return to her life once again
Hoping that she'd be forgiven.

But still the shadows of her thoughts
Entered her consciousness daily
And from the memories of all done
Unable to get away from completely.

The core of her spirit felt broken
She dreaded the dawn and the dusk
Each marking time yet status quo
Tormenting her soul, taking her trust.

How she yearned to feel released
From the heaviness that lay within
To put the past behind her firmly
And a new life to now here begin.

As days led into weeks and months
Eventually time did seem to heal
The acuteness of sorrow dampened
And some solace she began to feel.

The years have since marked changes
In her heart she is finally at peace
Forgiveness of self eventually came
As the lessons to learn appeased.

Thoughts at times do return to then
But less frequently and there're smiles
As she recalls special times and joys
Instead of the sadness and cries.

One day she knows that in reunion
She will be able to ask why it was
That he felt it necessary to go
Far away when they'd been so close.

She will ask what she could've done
What had been the prompt for his act
But for now, she is content to 'be'
Not by her ruminations attacked.

As with all sorrow there is some joy
Soon or in the future beyond it seems
Hope eternal returns in waves to her
Like the ebb and flow of the sea.

Kate Brumby

Yolani

I wish I could sing
I would sing seas of songs
And if only I could write
I would write a million letters
That would fill pages of books.

If only I could come
I would cross a thousand worlds
I would pass by millions of cities
I would withstand colds in the seas
I would overcome thorns in the jungles
I would interlock shores of oceans.

I remember you and tears come
You were the relief drink of my heart
You were the only shade for my soul
You were the only thought in my mind
You were the only refuge of my fear
And now,
You're gone.

I feel and touch your cold pictures

I remember and hear your memories

I tang and miss your owned cologne

But it's hard to learn

That you're gone.

Brian Ngusale

The Pain

You would never know it
The constant pain I feel
Because in the light of day
It almost isn't real.

Sure, I'll play, I'll laugh
I'll sing some songs
But the pain is always lurking
Because it's been here all along.

And when the darkness comes
With its all-consuming power,
It slowly takes my soul
Hour by dreadful hour.

But they tell me that I am strong enough
They swear that it gets better
They say, if you can just hold out
And bear this stormy weather.

They tell me, you will be happy one day.

All you need to do is fight

But what they seem to forget

Is after each day comes the night.

And so I act along

I play my part

While this crushing darkness

Slowly breaks my heart.

Simphiwe Sihawu Dlamini

You and I

When I am stranded and all alone
With no place to call home
You are who I think about
As my mind fills with doubt.

The emotion flood raging in my soul
Moving every direction but towards the goal
Sadness envelopes every fiber of my body
Knowing you're with a new lover.

Trying to step out of fear and regret
In the end all we find is a lifelong debt
Seeing you, arm in arm, with a selfish someone
Deep inside you know is not the one.

How can we stop the magnetic tugging?
Most of the time it leads us to drugging
Knowing that it would not be right
My throat constricts; for my breath I must fight.

True passion is so hard to find
When we do; it leaves us blind
All that could be is left in the past
For in our souls, we know this will never last.

Stepping out of our skin one more time
We end up venturing down a thin red line
Where honesty was never the question
And the lies became our greatest obsession.

We dream about being perfect, just us two
Of being something beyond beautiful
Where our bodies can be intertwined
A place we kiss our fears goodbye.

It is you that helps me stay strong
Even though you left me for another
Dreams left to shatter in millions of pieces
And led to believe the human race is a sad species.

I wish we could start this all over again
To erase this scary and lonesome end
Looking in the mirror though I feel no shame
Knowing I am a forsaken human being.

Venessa Valdez

Butterfly

Butterfly, you remind me of my beloved

You come into my garden

Unannounced

And leave on your own

After a few flutterings

And random flights.

And you don't stay near me

At least not on my request

Like my beloved,

But again, you come back

Unexpected like my beloved

Under the spell of my love.

I wait for minutes, hours and days

Just to see you flutter

Beside me

Like my beloved, you stay on for a while.

Even though briefly

To satiate my eyes.

Surendra Sahu

◆ ◆ ◆

"We try to be happy
We attend one more funeral
The gases and smoke from the
burning body remind us of our
end"

-Surendra Sahu-

◆ ◆ ◆

The Shepherd Boy Speaks of a Bird

To the right or left

The north or south

This bird won't fly away

It won't sing a song

Or dread a poking eye.

It rolled down the mountain

And turned down some grapes

And bouquet of fig

Maybe it once shook its tail

When she had a lover.

But lovers come and go

Some come in spring

Some come in autumn

Lovers must surely come.

Cry no more, fly away

Break a twig from the trees

And get frisky in the sky

But bird won't fly away!

Neith'r will she sing a song
Or stretch her wings
Like she's proud of them
She stands and falls.

Then over the hills, it rolled
Through the mud
And through the bank
Of river Limpopo.

Again she stands, again she falls
Over sun-cooked stones
The Shepherd boy is dismay'd

Little bird, won't you fly away?!
I need no flight, it cried
There's no reason to sing
If my voice won't go far
To wake my mother.

Ebom Tobe Churchill

Parasite of My Pain

Parasite of my pain
You have ended your play
In this world's dull display
With death's iron appearing laughter
Winning the fight thereafter.

In obedience to the cold call
I have seen your figure fall
To several feet under
Where you will no more wander.

Where you will no longer win
Your way of life within
But blessed should you be
For the life you lived like a bee
Oh! Parasite of my pain!

Brian Ngusale

Don't Cry for Me

Oh, will you stop crying for me?
I do not feel your tears, I swear.
Just take your love and let me be.
I'm an owl, too ugly to be dear.

When the sun shines, it shows
The big blisters on my body
I go to bed in anguish
But save your lull'bies when I sleep.

Your care is like a ruthless task
A prying nose, a watching eye
Keep it and do not ever ask
Why I fail'd to soar so high.

Don't love me; I don't love you too
There's no hope, but don't lend me one
I bear no result to show to you
Pass the stick to another, I'm done.

'Gnore the endless tears in my eye
It's my pain; I'm the hurting one
I long to hide my shame and die
When you won't notice I'm gone.

Your love is my worst fear and foe
It makes my failure stand in pride
Or love me if you talk'd with those
That help'd Job in ruins and divide.

Don't hold my hands when it is dark
I'm used to loneliness and fear
You can only grease my elbow
By the standing walls of Jericho.

Don't cry, for I don't cry for you
I'm sorry I can't make you proud
I shriek among those defeat'd few
That hide beneath the joyous crowd.

From the ones you love, sieve me out
And for once, you'd be free from shame
And I grant you will stop to frown
When you forget about my name.

A black and white TV I am
Beaten black and blue by trend
Well, I will sit and keep calm
As I crave to see my tragic end.

Fate has conspired against me
I don't count, not to mention my creed
Who will I call to set me free?

When not an ear my voice can feed.

I can't be loved in this place
I've gone here and there
I've looked in people's face
But there's no acceptance here
Where have I not gone seeking peace?

I'm used to hurt and heart breaks
My life is a storm, I'm rolling in dust
Thus, my heart has a firm crust
I'm covered in stone flakes

I've burnt more bridges than I can count
I don't want to be reached
I want to drown this time
As if I have a choice.

Naked, I stand under the cloud.
I see no God, no sun, no silver lining
Maybe grief has blindfolded my eye
Mayb' no one hears I scream so loud
Crying.

Ebom Tobe Churchill

Life's Journey

What is life?

Some activity, work and work

Desires remain in the womb of mind

They get fulfilled

Like flowers bloom in succession.

We search for the meaning of life

And happiness

Frustrations stare at us

We try to be happy

We attend one more funeral

The gases and smoke from the burning body

Remind us of our end.

We resolve for a moment

To be good and virtuous and useful

We must toil in our gardens ceaselessly

A new crop, a new bloom

Awaits our admiring and grateful eyes.

Surendra Sahu

Cigarette

As my fingers reached the tip,

My lips hugged it

While you were at the back of my mind,

I inhaled to the fullest.

I was on the verge of suffocation

I held every cloud as long as I could

Until I needed to breathe

I had to exhale,

To let go every memory of you.

But you let a part of me drift with you

Yes, I was able to smoke you out

Releasing a puff of anxiety

I knew you were killing me

Yet, I took another puff

I knew you were toxic

Yet, you were my favorite.

Simran Munot

Unprepared

The room felt cold and empty
Yet somehow, I felt his touch
In every moment I missed him
Emotions surged and rushed.

I felt depleted and dejected
Afraid of my feelings inside
Not wanting to be with others
Hiding the tears that I cried.

My solitude I needed to face
To somehow realize he has gone
And that he'll never return here
No matter how I yearn or long.

I know deep down I can do it
But perhaps today is not the time
So soon, so soon to lose him
Too soon to be brave to now try.

I toss in turmoil and agitation
Not knowing how to be, what to do
Fearing rejection or dismissal
If I now reach out to you.

Nothing I've known prepared me
For any of this, and of his passing
No one can help me fully here
Even you for whom I am calling.

But maybe, perhaps you'll save me
As I feel my being falling away
And just stay and hold me
Not always but just for today.

Tomorrow, tomorrow will be better
I will be more ready to go on
But today, please respond, please
Today I need you, I need my Mum.

Kate Brumby

Silent Love

Love has happened to me
But I dare not express it to you
For the tempests of love will engulf us
And we will be defamed.

All true love is silent
It expresses in only actions
But I am afraid to show
My love in my actions
For the loveless world shall
Frown over ours.

If chance brings us face to face
We will look at each other
For a moment
And then turn away
As if we were strangers.

But love is cruel and ruthless
It shall torment us
But only a sweet torment
Accompanied by moments of bliss
As there is day after the night
So there shall be meetings after partings.

Love is not within our control
Howsoever we try to suppress
It shall raise its fiery head
Like a hit cobra
Or a healthy seed plant on good soil.

Surendra Sahu

I Dream of a World

I dream of a world

A world where
Questions were answered and
Answers were questioned.

A world where
Roses were pure and without thorns.

A world where
Sadness received only love and affection.

A world where
Miracles were seen more than daylight.

A world where
Never was replaced with forever.

A world where
Our eyes could see through
The dark of the night.

A world where
Passion lived in us more than ever.

A world where
You and I would last forever.

A world where
Knowledge was worth more than gold and silver.

A world where
Love was sacred and endless as the seas.

A world where
God was the man's only path.

A world where
Hope was the foundation
Of the world we knew.

A world where
Beauty was seen everywhere
For I dream of that world.

Simphiwe Sihawu Dlamini

Sun

I.

When I rose at dawn

My eyes I turned to your gown

And saw the night's last breath

Taking its departure from earth

And it silently left.

I washed my face

And sat at the verandah

I waited for your embrace

In the cold valley of Yolanda.

I hanged on my feet

And hoped only you'll be up

Before the end of the fleet

But by noon you didn't even pop

And the day silently sunk.

For a hundred hours I recited

The first day of your decline

And on the fifth day I was lifted

To make a call via your line.

Your hearth was so weak sun

Even my voice you couldn't remember

And upon my implore of your song
You said tomorrow you knew not if ever.

My garden was deeply wilted
With weakness which was worn
And my brewed dew impatiently waited
For your light out to its home.

It's for you sun that I would pray
To have your feet well again
That would lead to bringing the ray
And have you smile down again
Upon my looking unto your eyes.

II.

Further in haste
The day was inclining
At the heart of the forest
An owl was crying
So I waited for your light
After that cold and deep night.

I walked out in burden
To where no tree stood
And across the fenceless garden
There roared a moony mood.

The sky was pale

With a circling Columbus cloud

That the whole way it bereaved

Your renowned and only road.

Like a dream I did persist

Saliently inclining my calls

Wondering whether the East

Truly sealed her walls.

As the winds cheerlessly ran

Across the ray less lane

And the shadows sightlessly followed

Their Lords silently sorrowed.

III.

My soul circles over you

Like a dog following a clue

I have barred as hard

It's voice from being heard.

But whenever you sever into my eyes sun

My heart inside runs insane

No matter how hard I try

I learn it's to me that I lie.

The love I learnt, not taught
I wonder at what price it'll be bought
For I've laid it in deep silence
But it's set again before I distance.

It has been like sweetening the sea
Or rather running over the sea
For you're the only floor unto
At last I'll land onto
You're the only hero in the sea salt
That'll overpower my sweetening might.

IV.

My moments have grown snowy
And my world very lonely
My weakness has turned vigorous
And strength I have not in generous.

My soul is no longer a city
Of sweet songs selecting serenity
My laughter is no longer even the vice
Of the priceless joy heaped into a voice.

My eyes I have turned high
Searching the clouds for you to sigh
My knees are bowed to the east
Praying hard for the fall of the mist.

My whole world is enclosed in cold

Because of your absence you gold

My heart is unyoked in yawn

As I walk and talk alone.

V.

I have waited for you

And tried to face your view

But you've come and gone

And I'm still alone.

You have walked across the sky

Having seen you I'll not lie

For even in the world there is

Your steps where you didn't miss.

I have seen you jog downtown

Across noon since your bitter dawn

I have even climbed Everest

To whisper to you in your nest.

But sun you don't have an ear

For I have sung this whole year

Until I have grown horns of fear.

I have written you letters on papers

But you haven't even picked your spectacles

I'll fight no longer for thee

For now, I'm like a mother bee

And there's no more wave I can do

To have my heart cross to yours too.

VI.

It's hard to return

The hand I had outstretched

The step I had raised

The tongue I had rolled

The ears I had harked

The eyes I had set.

It's hard oh sun!

To lock my open heart

To close my unsealed soul

To bind my unbowed mind

To let my tapped hope

Its hard sun, I say!

VII.

Hold onto your hands, sun

So I may rise from the sand

For you're noble and royal

I can't face your denial.

35

I will run and range

Escaping your strange revenge

Allow my soul to be at nap

Before my face you slap.

Reign in your lids miss sun

And allow me a lesson to learn

Light not the entire sky

And leave me the endarkened pie.

Understand oh! Miss mysterious

For how will I be serious?

When the whole world I elude.

VIII.

Indeed, it has been time

That has seen us bedraggle and rhyme

But this evening how am I

To face this east straight in the eye?

I see you had been mine

When you're lost and missed you like wine

As in my heart you imported civility

And in my mind planted credulity.

I know it has been time

When my soul you etherized with lime

As I followed you to the mouth of River Kiang
And sang for you without even a single slang.

I learn it has been hollow
When our whole world sank into sorrow
After you had spread your absence in the sky
As it turned to be you and I.

Indeed it has been dark
When our heart strengthened on the shivering bark
As the waves fracas our ways
As our vows were flayed in the dog days.

I hear it has been long
Ever since in the world we belonged
I entreat from dilatory enmity
As I entitle your eulogy eternity.

Brian Ngusale

The Tender Moment

The desire is born

And the whole body

Catches fire

Passive looks and thoughts

Reign the preceding hours

Resulting in the senseless jump

A struggle continues for mutual satisfaction

When 'the final point' comes

An agitated body finds rest

For a couple of hours

Or perhaps days

After a few deep breaths

Of satisfaction.

Surendra Sahu

Looking for You

I look for you

In the scorching mid-day sun

I look for you

In pounding rains

Hoping you will come out

In your balcony.

I look for you

In freezing winter winds

To quench the hunger of my eyes

Just a glimpse

Just a meeting of eyes

Just a little solace.

To our impossible love

To our pre-ordained love

To our souls

Love is a mere chance

Strangers become intimate

As if they have known for many births.

Love is not a union of smartness with beauty

Love is between ordinary folk

Imperfect and unlikely ones.

Surendra Sahu

The Mask

My smile hides my tears
My laugh hides my screams
It's been this way for years
Things aren't as they seem.

I always seem so happy
With not a care in the world
But sadly, you should know,
Many things go untold.

Nobody really knows me
They only know my cover
But I wish I could let it free
Let them know what's under.

But instead, I practice

My smiles in the mirror

Then the next thing I do is

Make my fake laugh clearer.

What is wrong? You need help?

Is all they will ask

So I have decided

To live behind a mask.

Simphiwe Sihawu Dlamini

Realm of Darkness

As the evening twilight fades away
The sky is filled with stars, invisible by day
There is a realm to which I go
Where I am free to be myself
A secret hell only I know
A place I allow my darkness to show.

I need freedom to explore my thoughts
Regurgitate my past as it continues to haunt me
Relive the nightmare of frightening times
Being beaten till my breath no longer existed.

This realm of darkness is my best friend
By my side till the very end
Reminding me of being touched
In places an eight-year-old never should be.

Replaying memories in my head
Stripped down to bare skin
Bent over and aggressively tied to a tree
Brutally having unknown things
Forced deep inside me

I felt pain I've never felt before
Pain that left me screaming.

This is a realm where darkness shows
The scars on my arms and legs
Imprinted and telling of their stories
A constant reminder of all my pains
Which are open and still bleeding.

This realm of darkness I can't escape
For it is part of who I am
Reminding me of pains no one can relate to
But ones I've grown so fond of
Broken relationships, feeling inadequate
Having a past turn me bitter.

Sticking needles into my veins
As I drift off to another realm
One I like much better.

Becoming a whore
To satisfy my next fix
Doing things other people
Can't even fathom.

This is a realm where thoughts are free
Imagining slow torture
Of those that have hurt me
Things I'll never be able to speak of.

This is a place only I can go
Where the sky is filled with stars, invisible by day
As the evening twilight fades away
A place I'm very fond of
Where I am free to be myself.
This is my realm of darkness.

Venessa Valdez

Words Are Not Enough

If I was a painter
I would have used the sky
As a canvas
To paint my heart
For words are not enough
To describe the darkness
Eating up my soul.

I would have painted
A boy that keeps walking
Into the wrong path
And seeking sunrise
From the west
But I can't paint it all.

I'd have sung a song too
If I was a singer
I'd sing by the roadside
Everyday till I finish
The last verse of my song
Which will break the hearts
Of the ears that hear them.

We don't finish singing
Said a little toad
I sing everyday
Yet I cannot bare my heart
Sometimes you can't hear
The sound of your voice
Then you wonder if you died
Or if you still have a choice.

My soul is out of stock
It's been bought by devil
Though I didn't get a receipt
But it doesn't bother me
There's a crack in my frame
Particles fall off my figure
As I cry every day.

The sun has taken an oath
Swearing my clothes won't dry
Everyday makes me sadder
And I wear the garment of fear
I am a boy with bruised toes
On a Christmas Eve.

If you are reading this

I've made a bargain with Satan

Don't stay crying for me

I prefer life when I'm dead

Farewell to handkerchiefs

I wouldn't be cleaning tears

Or have to cry anymore.

My head is a diagram of ruins

It barely bothers my soul

I'll die when next I shut my eye

And I'll be laid close to my mother

So she can see her boy at last

In a place God cannot reach.

Ebom Tobe Churchill

Languid

Awoken from desperation I had thought
The brokenness of sleep at an end at last
Yet with the light of the morning there
I felt spent, body and mind without rest.

So many nights of sleep staccatos
Jumping up with the quietest of noise
Shadows appearing to outline a form
Dreams of hearing his reassuring voice.

No yearnings and longings satisfied
The coldness of hope upon sheets is sure
Alone and without console of his touch
Seems like my new norm forevermore.

Bereft of anyone truly understanding
All too busy with their own lives to care
Many a day I deliberately remained alone
Energy seeping out like a slow puncture.

Void of courage or interest to venture

Nothing of the outside world wanted by me

The only way, the one resolution

Was the falling into an endless sleep.

Kate Brumby

Spoils of Abweido

I followed the less-travelled routes
Threw my life in the air
Hoping to catch it by chance
Because the risk was worth it
For Abweido, to say the least.

I went naked before Benue
I worshipped before the evening winds
That consoled broken fishermen
At the bank of Zambezi,
Because I prayed for Abweido
And pledged allegiance
Should they help find my queen.

I saw the moon go to bed
At the other side of the ocean
I felt answers would come as currents
Like bedspread on the waters,
Even in glee, my heart was trembling
Like a boy masturbating in the woods
I kept wishing and waiting
For Abweido.

When the clime played hide and seek
Pushing the dust to wherever

I took the other way untouched
And unscorned by dust,
At least I knew for sure that nature
Wouldn't even disrespect Abweido
Her beauty is beyond compare.

I saw travelers with a dame held high
She was the fairest in their clan,
I told them the story of Abweido
And many affirmed they knew her
Her eyes were known to bully the sun
And tales of her beauty made their dame
Look like a dirty rag,
They sent me away for the disdain
Suffered by the woman they adored.

My legs tried dry sands of Saharah
Compass became my only companion
Here and there I journeyed,
Like waters exchanging pleasantry
Forced by irrigation in harmattan
I could journey to the end of the world
Just to find Abweido,
And consider the tedious task
Less painstaking.

And by all means I avoided
The path that reeked of the songs

Of Kofi Awoonor's sorrows
Because I could bet my life
That Abweido's beauty could not be
In a place shared with travails.

And then to a little town
Over the hills could bear witness
Of my nostalgia,
The people were dismayed
As they carried a dead young athlete
Immediately I left them,
Taking the opposite way,
Because in a land of mourning
You shouldn't find Abweido.

Abweido would have searched for me
She would have waited like a woman
Expecting a child,
They would have told her I had died
But Abweido knew I wouldn't die
Maybe she didn't know where to be
So I could find her.

I climbed the highest mountain
With the effort just enough
To walk down a slop
My veins flowed with valor
As I searched for Abweido

I spent my strength happily
At least Abweido was worth more --
More than anything.

I followed a few songbirds
Back to whence they emerged
Because I suspected they took
Singing tutorials from Abweido
Those with beauty weren't left out
Because Abweido should be seen
In a place blossoming with splendor.

I met every perfect thing
Forests of fascinating flowers
I investigated the bees
Guessing they sucked nectar
From her blood,
I searched every form of sweetness
Because Abweido wouldn't dwell
In a place other than that.

Onto the sky, I set my grieving gaze
To see if there was another sun
A brighter sun, Abweido's face
I repeated this at every dawn
I prayed to the gods of the sky
To give me a day with Abweido
And in return, take my life,

Yet I'd consid'r it the fairest deal

From time immemorial.

I could not find my fair mistress

In a place where beauty lies

So I inclined to spoils and the faulty

Fractions, and everything that dies

Then I saw a huge gathering

Where worn wounded women were weeping

And the men struggling to shake off

The grieve from their head.

I saw Abweido, my Abweido sleeping—

No, not sleeping, she was lying alone

Defeated and defied by the hand of death

My beautiful Abweido was dead

And her beauty abandoned her.

Ebom Tobe Churchill

◆ ◆ ◆

His wings and his heart shattered
All joy and reason were now lost
One moment of irresponsibility
Was being paid at full cost"

-Kate Brumby-

◆ ◆ ◆

Depression

She's a girl who didn't
Know herself well.
She seemed a happy,
Joyful child very
Different though.

This child lived a life
A life of silence
She did not have many to
speak to
Not much to say.

Death, cutting, depression
Was a part of her life
That was all it was
Death, Cutting and
Depression.

She was ignored
By the same people
That were supposed to love her
She was always alone.

Her parents thought she

was a mistake

A thing that never should be

A disgrace that shouldn't have occurred.

She was never loved by no one

She was 'a waste' she has told herself

She asks *Do I try to disturb the life of*

good people?

And then she no longer feels

She no longer puts herself

In pain and misery

She puts herself out of it

For once, she felt good

She felt normal and still.

Simphiwe Sihawu Dlamini

Mary

We loved that merry
Of running down the river
And imagined being in the ferry.
You were my mighty Mary
For you were forever and ever
We loved that merry.

You're my long-distance glory
Having lived in me like a liver
And imagined being in the ferry.
Years are distance Mary
For they set I from you, my reliever
We loved that merry.

When our ways were weary
We once prayed facing the river
And imagined being in the ferry.
I'll surname our times of yore, Mary
To engender our life by the river
We loved that merry
And imagined being in the ferry.

Brian Ngusale

Bloodshed

Trapped in a trance

Ignoring the indignant eye

Your heart keeps falling

I'm the eager one that won't stop calling.

Have I pushed you too far away?

Soaked your skin in my blood today

Here to encounter how your life shall end

Yet then again, a new one will begin.

Look deep inside as two comets collide

Your standing here by my side

Filling me with ample pride

But here I am, caught in a landslide.

Do I come inside and attempt to mend

All your anguish and lifelong pains?

When time and time again

Many have tried yet all have failed.

She lied to you and did you wrong

In due time you will stand strong

Carry on,

Life is not gone.

Loneliness, emptiness won't leave
But soon enough the pain shall go
Leaving you with a brand-new soul.

Intrigued by a revelation
You reveal what you long to conceal
I do not understand it
How could I have been so wrong?

You opened your heart
It started a spark
Made me complete
Yet now I can't think.

You broke my heart
And play these head games
Left me caught in a battle
Between right and wrong.

Encapsulated
How does one carry on?

My skin is thick
Yet still it drips
The blood so red
Flowing from my veins
It's beyond comforting.

You ripped my heart right in two.

Pushed needles in my veins

Till I became numb

And started to turn blue.

The wicked laugh echoes in my ears

Brought back to life from your greatest fears

So, it is I who has the last laugh

For you cannot kill me when I'm already dead.

My eyes are bloodshot

My body aches

I have a feeling you were

My greatest mistake.

Torn away from all I knew,

It is just a matter of time

Before lost and lonely

Is all you will know too.

Left alone to die

Forever forsaken

As I walk arm in arm

Holding the arm of no one else.

Venessa Valdez

Invisible Difference

Walking home I saw you

You didn't see me

I passed right in front of your eyes

You could have smelled my

Strawberry, scented hair

I saw the stick

You did too.

But you didn't see me

I was watching you

Not watching me

I tripped, fell

The gravel came up too fast

I saw the streams of blood running

Down my leg

In the newly formed gravel crevices

Before I felt the searing pain.

But you didn't see me

I could have died, and you would not have seen me

Because I was different from you

You would not have seen me.

Simphiwe Sihawu Dlamini

◆ ◆ ◆

"My smile hides my tears
My laugh hides my screams
It's been this way for years
Things aren't as they seem"

-Simphiwe Sihawu Dlamini-

◆ ◆ ◆

Passage to Sadelina

More than the potency of sunshine

More than the Achilles' heel of divine

More than the cold of Neptune

Does your eulogy in me subdue?

For if it's to mourn, I've mourned

Like a sapphire near a rear window

If it is to long, I've longed

Like a widower or a widow

If it is to pray, I have prayed

Like a puritan who is afraid

If it is doom, I've been doomed

Like a sunless day at noon.

We had to shyly say Sadelina

Goodbye, we said oh! Sadelina.

Now I hear a crying owl

I dreamt of a dancing dog

I see a sea of darkness

The yoke of lunacy broke in me

I walk the fields of Asian oceans

Immune to sinking and the unfolding cold

I sing the songs of Hiawatha

I dance the plays of Sir Shakespeare

Calling you back, excuse me rather

My heart's bleeding from a shaking fear

As my deepest dullness displays

For my mats of happiness are soiled

Since my empire of life has coiled

In my independence from you, Sadelina.

Brian Ngusale

Surplus

The last thing you said was you'd had enough
Closing the door, you shut me completely out
No interest in what I had to say in reply
You did not hear me in anguish shout.

Left without opportunity to respond at all
All communication cut in one fell swoop
Abandoning and rejecting our joint vows
That you pledged to me, and I to you.

As I look back upon our time together
Nothing of it now makes any sense
Of all that I had come to rely upon gone
I wonder now did you only act, pretend?

What of the shared smiles and laughter
Were they a charade, some kind of game?
Was it my failing looks that changed all?
Or regular medication taken for pain?

So many questions I have, yet no answers
No opportunity granted; no grace bestowed
The reasons as to why you really went,
Only you and you alone really know.

I am surplus to your requirements
Of no further use in your pompous life
You are without honor of a gentleman
Walking out so decisively from I your wife.

Angry? Am I angry? That comes nowhere near!
I am enraged, but more so desolate and bereft
Though you are able to dismiss the years gone
I cannot and don't wish them to ever forget.

Tears stream down my cheeks in sadness
My heart is broken, shattered into shards
Thoughts are rushing around my mind
Wondering why you blatantly me disregard.

In time perhaps my wounds will heal over
Yet I doubt this will be the case at all
Everything changed in that one single moment
You said you'd had enough and closed the door.

Kate Brumby

My Beloved

Let me love you from afar

Let me suffer

Let me depend on fate

Let me wait

For that chance encounter.

I did not plan for you

You came like an unexpected cold breeze

From the gap in the window.

So let me see what

Chance brings us.

Let me be satisfied with fates portion.

Let me not be mad like a true lover.

And let me wait

And see how you come

Into my life.

Surendra Sahu

◆ ◆ ◆

"Nobody understands my anguish,
My pain
It's as though I'm not even real"

-Venessa Valdez-

◆ ◆ ◆

Dreaming

Slowly disintegrating in this god-forsaken world

I'm lost in an uncharted sea of confusion

Tell me, what in life is real?

Please say, reality is not merely an illusion.

Life's a long, long road

Where, with one wrong turn

There's no safe return

Too many bridges end up getting burned.

Farther and farther down I fall

The walls are closing in and keep rising

Move forward, they always scream in my ear

But how, when nothing ever goes right?

There's not even a horizon to be a guiding light.

Trying to understand my wild thoughts

As you try to heal me and my afflictions

You're naïve to believe band-aids can mend

This black, ripped open, broken heart.

My thoughts are dark yet comforting

I watch my wrist slowly bleeding

Go into cardiac arrest

An intentional overdose

This is how I see my life ending.

Regrets keep coming in succession

Each, another addition to my depression

It's nobody's fault but my own.

I'm struggling to find a purpose

Yet to learn life's lessons

And live a life that's worth it.

Harder and harder to live with myself

When life's been cursed

And you're living in your own hell

It's damn hard to count your blessings

Or wish people well!

Life's a never-ending nightmare

I don't even know what's real

Maybe I'm just dreaming?

If I could only wake up

And keep my mind from screaming.

Venessa Valdez

Numb

My soul is trapped
In the clutter of my thoughts
I yell at my pen, pinch my hand
But there's no word this paper can comprehend.

Thoughts crave my inner creativity
They want to dance in the rain
They want to find a mysterious love potion
But my hands can't take them there.

I'm standing numb
As my thoughts sleep
Inside my feeble heart.
I'm either trapped inside myself
Or lost in an entangled world.

Simran Munot

Ndidi (a dirge)

Edumeku,

Can you see your child?

Lying cold like a drenched hand

Waving byes to Harmattan

Can you see how those eyes

Have lost their colors?

She has gathered the firewood

She has left the farm for good.

But does it not bother you

That the firewood is not dry?

The rains just started

Or can you not see the blue sky?

Her eyes still had mist so fresh

For the sun had barely spoken

Does it not bother you?

You should've wait'd for May rash hours

Before you said your sad goodbyes!

My mother is the morning dew

Quite allergic to the evening sun

What does it matter anyway?

As if she had a choice!

Ndidi,

Maybe you meant nothing to God
You were just an unlucky lily
Left to the mercy of raging flood
Atop tough thorns down the valley.

But since He left you, how could you
Do the same, sweetheart, to me?
You thought it was all about you?
Every sand poured on you, b'ried me!

You shook off your fine cloak
Your sweet rainbow-velvety skin
Now, you melt away like an oak
As if you have the biggest sin.

What's there to await autumn falls?
Before your beauty starts dropping
At least, when May's breeze is hopping
Cotton fields won't mourn much fall'n bolls
Because they had substantial time
Before fate brought an alien clime.

In my heart hangs 'ternal curfew

It's silent while a cold breeze blows

My body is covered in dew

In my heart every day, it snows.

When blueberries sprout in springy hues

There goes the locusts or something alike

Beauty is the preamble of bad news

As you bask in glee, do expect a strike.

Beautiful things attract despair

And s'ddenly fade into thin air

But sun is fine, yet forever strong

Why won't Ndidi sing same song?

Maybe the sun conspires with fate

Nothing is safe under its gaze!

There's nothing good about the sun

Because the world still remains dark

The light it uses to bright'n each dawn

Comes to see tears turn our face mark.

See that area under the sands

Yes, right below lies a treasure

A flower trapped in the hands
Of great woes that time can't measure.
B'neath the weed lies laughter, lives love
Whose hands have been cut by him 'bove
How can the senseless weevil see,
That they bite the hands that fed me?

Let hundred years come, meet me here
This despair will only look so new
That's if you hope that time will clear
This loss, whose time is never due.

When did a dove turn a cricket,
That she should lay beneath the soil?
My mother doesn't live in my heart
She's under the soil as you so wish
And the beauty God claims to be his art
Bleeds on the canvas, while he watches
And does nothing like a fool.

My despair is the boundless Savanah
And my pain heavier than baobab tree
My thoughts are like twisted trees of guava
I can't paint; I'm not poet enough to spill
The agonies in my soul.

I checked on you, I called upon you

Like calling birds on Christmas times

You turned away, yet, I felt your presence

Won't you answer this call, save my wailing?

Hasn't guilt overwhelmed my soul?

Hasn't tears turned a great sea?

What can tears do, my friend?

Can it float fragile feathers of fleas?

Or does it disturb the way of heaven?

Does prayer make God hiss?

That he ignores them every time

Well, it doesn't matter anymore

Nothing can bring back my mother.

How could you, eyes of the sun

Close those eyes, which brighten

The afternoons and the dawn?

How could you, how could you tighten

Your heart against me, Ndidi?

Are you God that forsakes those

He claims to love and set free?

How could you trample on a rose;

The tender heart of your daughters?

Are you God that you should be wicked?

How can the tiny legs of a cricket

Become food to quench our hungers?

That's if your stay is as much

As cricket's toe, or your touch

As lasting as busy bodied dews

That make empty promises

To unsuspecting flowers.

How do you comfort a rabbit

Thrown to the rage of the sun?

How do you comfort a flower

Lying on a busy road?

How do you comfort a fowl

Whose chicks turned food for hawk?

The rabbit, the flower and fowl

Look at me from their ruins

How do we comfort you, Sir?

When your soul is like the shell

Of egg trampled by God?

I had everything I needed

And in a blink, I have nothing
Like a bat, I was thrown to darkness
Ev'ry second, my light quenches
Ev'ry day, I yield to pain.

My mother is the morning dew
Quite allergic to the evening sun
What does it matter anyway?
As if she had a choice.

It's not like I wanted everything
To go my way
But is it too much to ask
That the sun should shine
For one more day?

Ebom Tobe Churchill

For Mother!

Hurts

Hurts were hers alone - no one else's
The cuts upon her skin and heart
Self- inflicted by doubt and suspicion
Failure in accepting her own part.

To her these scars were caused
Not by herself - others had no care
And they cruelly twisted knives
Intentionally to humiliate her.

It was only when she became numb
As her life-giving blood ran dry
That she was able to understand
And work out the reasons why.

In the silence she unpicked her reality
Making sense of all she felt inside
And in that moment of realization
For her losses without gain cried.

Given up on so many aspirations
She had let go of her core dreams
Leaving herself without an anchor
Void of something in which to believe.

Then woken by His touch tender
She all at once was able to see again
And taking His hand offered there
She knew on Him to now depend.

Her whole being felt renewed now
The scars would in time heal and go
And with the lessons learnt from Him
She would to others reach out and show.

He and she would be together always
Life and living with joy and love
On this the earth of her home now
Through to eternity in His home above.

Kate Brumby

Visions of Mother and Fetus

Yet dark and sightless eyes that never sleep
Amidst the starkly placid, endless wake
Of faceless dreams, obscured by secrets deep
And awful presence that darkness can make.
What sheer and dormant form becomes this hour
Empowered by feelings henceforth never known
By mind and hand, held dearly for their being?

A tearless vision the dark vast has grown
Looms blue and helpless from tragic foreseeing,
Rapt and nameless in the nights chilling peace;
Whose ceaseless wonder shone upon your cheek,
A blameless color, of which the varied moons
Of future, moved by lone, lost ponds would seek
Crippled in all beauty, and will, which it swoons
At the anguish of long, uncertain days.

A faith which prays on a painless minute
Far from the beaming, unnatural glare
Bearing mortal pain and its infinite plight
Born still, where the bright but lifeless stare.

Venessa Valdez

The Epileptic Emotion

As the midnight approaches

Memories of past love

Seize me

Two deep draughts of air

Escape my heated nostrils

As my eyes look into them

In my faithful but cheap mirror

A weary body

Pulls shutters of mind

A haze remains

Of past pleasures and pains

Driving me into a stone-dead sleep.

Surendra Sahu

The Day of Silence

They all lay arms stretched
Some holding bloodied machetes
Some heads lying under heavy stones
Some lay eyes opened
And blood was spread like sand in the sea.

No door or window was opened
Some only were broken
No breakfast was made
And no milk was milked
And only the cows broke their manger.

Little children who survived
Peeped through the broken doors
And they trusted none
As they hid by the slumber.

Souls knelt, lined in heaven
Some bowed with shame
Some crying with guilt
Some still rude with anger
Some confused with misunderstanding.

Brian Ngusale

My Tear

I am your tear
I make you look weak
Minding my own business
Strolling down your cheek.

I am your tear
I mock you with shame
It all ends
With your cutting game.

When you're done your game
You still see me
Wandering down your face
With no sense of glee.

You try everything
To get me away,
But all you do
Is cry all day.

Then the next day
And the day after that
You still see me
Resting on your face
With no sense of glee.

I am your tear
I have no bliss
For that's my position
To give you a sorrowful kiss.

Simphiwe Sihawu Dlamini

Song of a Bat

Let me love you now

Beside a fresh April tree

So I'd still hold you in Octob'r

When your waist bead is dusty

And your nipples are forced to bow

To pressures of two decades or three

And when your beauty-drunk eyes get sob'r

For it gets quite strong'r as you get mor' rusty.

Will I mean something to you

When I hold your body when snow

Falls on your skin, tame your youth blood?

But why then can't we be together, you fool?

I'd have loved to kiss thos' lips t'night, you know

And cause your bones to shake, your groin lips to flood?

And then a few other things I wouldn't talk about?!

But are you not ashamed

That someone loves you, yet he hurts?

Well, you aren't, and you shouldn't either

And of course, my feelings should be blamed

Some love *Pepsi*, while some of course do yoghurts.

What exactly does a man tell you

So they can hold you and make you stay?

What kind of eye sees your nakedness?

Are they made of sapphires and myrrh?

What words do lips emit?

Before they subdue yours in a kiss?

How do you find fires when the skies are blue?

Please, say so I can learn, by the gods, just say

Are they enchanted, the ears that hear you moan?

I learnt you are alone

But you can always meet someone

Somewhere better

But he may change your face

To a season where so much rain falls

But isn't that what you want,

To be abused, used, and held with disdain?

While I won't let you suffer the tiniest pain

Maybe pain has a way of pleasing you

Isn't that why you push me away

Because I can't hurt the things I love?

My whole body is a hearse

The sirens are blaring, my time beeping

My hormones honk like Nigerian Cops' van

That purposely show up when thieves leave

As I sing every day, the song of a bat,

You should also write a song or two

Let the lyrics tell of a broken man.

But why do you reject me?

What have I not done to let you be?

What have I not done to kiss you?

I've gone here and there

But I will not complain, you know

Besides the bat tried to find acceptance

As a rodent, or at least as a bird

I'll join him in the dark.

What do you think birds sing about?

How can you know when you're alone?

Curled up in your bed eating noodles

And telling friends you break hearts

Do you hear the whispers in the breeze?

How can you hear it when you walk alone?

Having no one to describe it to you!

There's a permanent tear-line on my face

You can easily mistake me for a cheetah

But really, I'm a bat, you know

Forgotten in the dark by someone.

The more I try to flutter as a butterfly

The more my feathers wash away

Yes, I am a moth, though I'm sad

I wish I was a butterfly or a bird

So I can be accepted and loved

The messages that make you laugh

When you touch your phone, eat *Pringles*
What are they made of, please say.

How do you get to smile so bright
When you are with someone else?
You pout your lips, jaws clench so tight
When I try to get your attention
Then you pretend your phone rings
Just so you can stay away
Even a murderer cannot bear
The weight of such rejection.

But I would still stand by you
When milk-toothed demons they call children
Drink the freshness of your breast
After making your stomach fluffy
You never loved big fluffy stomachs
What if I told you I wouldn't care
If your belly became so big and fluffy?
You still wouldn't give me a chance, right?
Because I'm too good to you.

Well I have red flags in my past
But you can salute my own flags
If you don't have any in your past
A day may come when my feelings
Will end faster than a student types
Account number to receive free funds.

This is an act of rejection like no other
One day you want me, to see me smile
And then that's it, you go away
You hate seeing me, by the gods!
But one can never get used to rejection
It always feels like breaking a coating sore.

It's not that you are the finest
But isn't that the sweetest,
The most fulfilling and peculiar?
Knowing you love a particular thing
That has prettier species
Isn't that the hook, the spark?
Isn't that what they mean when people talk about love?

I want to kiss you on every day
Peel off your panties, eat your groin, lips too
Honestly, I don't know what else to say

I'm guessing that's what lovers do
I'll buy you presents or at least make promises
Promises I'll fulfill this time, mark it
I shouldn't be writing these plenty verses
If you can identify fragments that fit.

I do not mean that you are blind
But then, can't you see we'd look good
If we were together?

You always leave me behind
You wouldn't if you understood
That we are tied to each other
Like an object and its shadow
Well maybe one can't touch the other
But it's alright.

She knows she's my shadow
I can't run away from her
I can't touch her either
I'll find my way into a brighter light
And I'll remember the songs
I used to sing for you.

But you are laughing with another
You make me feel he's better
More manly, taller and well-behaved
While I languish away in the dark
With my rejected arms around my shin
Singing like a lost swallow
This is the song of a bat
Who is tired of trying and trying
I don't love you baby.

Ebom Tobe Churchill

Dying

I can sit in front of a mirror

Look myself in the eye

As I watch this body

I'm trapped in slowly die

Surrounded by darkness

My only true friend

Dissolving into sand

That will slowly blow away

Maggots and spiders

Millions of hungry bloodthirsty bugs

Cover my body

Savoring every bite

My skin turns pale

My eyes sink in

I turn a washed-away grey

And begin to peel away

Layer by layer

Till I'm nothing but bone

Each slowly disintegrates

Turning into the dust

Which has become my fate.

Venessa Valdez

◆ ◆ ◆

"He no longer saw her innocence
Even when she behaved
Like silence
He no longer saw her innocence"

-Brian Ngusale-

◆ ◆ ◆

Temporar Munantur

They walked along languid in resolve
Two friends beneath the canopy,
Sunlight bursting fractioned
Accentuating nature's parquetry.

The footsteps of his and her echoed
The gentle swing of hands held loose,
No rush, no eagerness to leave at all
Barely wanting even time to move.

Content in one another's space
Completeness shared, no need for more,
Silent agreement without any words
This for them, their happy ever after.

Yet, not to be, the noise of change
Thoughts, dreams cast aloft adrift,
Taken in tragedy, sudden unexpected
One leaving the other to alone live.

Memories of days of solace and console
Like the creatures hidden from view,
The darkness of shade and shadow
Making the grief hard to see through.

Tempora mutantur, nos et mutamur in illis
Times are changed; we also are changed with them.

Kate Brumby

Songs for Benue

I've thrown countless cowries

To your infinite depth

Tired, I come before you

Not to request for lost children

You have digested in your bosom

I come to give you more

But not cowries this time

Or the wings of a rooster.

Stretch forth your tongue

And swallow me

Since you won't save me

From my horrors.

I want to die sailing

In your watery belly

Please, take me when I drown

To the breast of the moon

When it shines at night

To illuminate my grief

Or at least carry me on your back

To the edge of the world

So your tenants will know

Of a man that died trying.

And curse every bird

That takes a bite

From my weathered body

Unless they sing for me

And tell stories to those they see

Stories about my mother.

The boatmen, tell them thus

This man fought the winds

Though he's dead, but he dared

Tell them stories of my travails

And the nightmares that ate me up

Leave them in wonders

As you continue to journey

With my rumpled slain body

The world plays Russian roulette

With every existence on it

Tell them I was unfortunate.

At the point where you exchange

Pleasantry with Niger

Show my body around

Like a kill you are proud of

Should the merchants curse you

Curse them in return

School them to know

That life killed me

Every day I lived.

Don't leave me at the bank

Carry me in your arms

And bury me somewhere

Nobody can find.

Ebom Tobe Churchill

Her Spell

I just sit and gaze

At the hair that just swirl around

I become captive to her eyes

And caught by the infectious smile.

I could see the darkest dreams!

The hunger is voracious

Wants to consume every piece

Wants to tear apart and find something.

Something that fills her to the brim

But she can do nothing except

Destroying what she cannot have

I scream and yell

Yet everything in vain

As I am under her spell.

Simran Munot

Silent Prayer

Sprit above all, please.

Give me the strength
To be myself;
Not to be influenced unduly
By the worlds of others.

Give me the strength
To raise my body to its full strength
And stretch and realize.

Give me the strength
To do anything;
If only I believe.

Give me the strength
To pride and protect my priceless health
And give little attention to obsession to wealth.

Give me the strength

To live;

To think and reveal

To express and feel.

Give me the strength

To have hope.

For without hope my spirit would die

For without hope my dreams would die.

For I seek the strength

That will give me power to change

My thoughts, attitude and feelings.

Simphiwe Sihawu Dlamini

I Thought

I never thought you would come
With me to our home
When I said we'll walk
Slowly on foot and not talk.

I never thought you wouldn't fear
To continue after shedding a tear
And continue following the path
After healing a broken heart.

I never thought you would stand
To face our smoldering kitchen
And follow my little sister
At dawn to fetch water.

I never thought you would withstand
The fall of rain
On the roof of our house
Against the window of our house.

I never thought you would learn
The only tongue that I first learnt
And in such a time call me so
To pass a secret before visitors.

I can't imagine you really stayed
Near me for all these days
I never thought it would be you
With wrinkled face and failing voice.

Brian Ngusale

Forgetting the Beloved

It would seem I've forgotten you
But I recollect you in solitude
Our first kiss
Our feverish bodies
Embracing under the hot shower
In the afternoon.

The wetting of the underwear
Of a sex-starved body
I applied color to your face
On Holi.

Your supple, fresh and teenage beauty
Our moments of togetherness
My resolve to forget you
And the fact I'm loving you more by the day
And forever.

You are the cause of my verse

You are the topic of my poetry

You are the why of my prizes

You are the substance

Of my life.

You are the queen of my thoughts

And the muse of my mid-night poetry

You are my joy

You are my pain

You are my world

Yet you are nothing to me

In the eyes of the world.

Surendra Sahu

Timing

It's not easy to know when to ask
Nor what to ask for to even know,
The confusion within me here
Seems with veracity to grow.

In one moment, I feel in control
The next I am bewildered, forlorn,
And the one I really want nearby
Is he for whom I cry and mourn.

I had thought I was strong enough
As with tears I shed I show bravery,
But in truth I am at a complete loss
Without him here beside me.

I long for just a few moments
To hold his hand and feel him close,
To speak with him my thoughts
To hear his wisdom and his voice.

It is not possible for a reunion
Ahead my lover, he has gone,
And so, I must find a way - my way
To alone without him, live on.

I will take console that he's at peace
No longer hurting or in any pain,
I will endeavor to survive here
Until in Heaven we meet once again.

I will try to hold on, I really will
To all of his love -it gives me strength,
And not wish my own life away
Though I wish it were at an end.

I may not know when to ask for help
Or know what kind of help I need,
So, I end by saying just this, reader
Please, please pray for me.

Kate Brumby

Tell Dieye

I am a Big Island
Of mangrove forest
This is my own soul
You see as swampy waters
There's music sometimes
From tired birds
That could give an arm
To die before me.

I've accepted this failure
This apparel, this misfortune
No man has ever spit out sugar
But since I won't get any
Let it be like that
I've worn the black dress.

There's a big tree in my belly
You can cut leaves for herbs
If you want to cook sorrow
My time has long passed
Since I was twenty-four
It doesn't bother me, friend.

Blisters in the heart are countless
Like Likes on Kylie Jenner's post

How many can I give my eyes?

I behold my affliction, own it

Like a communion, I drink, numbly

As if I have a choice.

My body is a mountain

Of great salty waters

Gradually, I drip through my eyes.

But I won't drip forever

You won't find me

When you come tomorrow.

What then is happiness?

Why do I force it down my throat?

Why do I struggle with it?

When I keep drowning?

I do not know how to swim.

There's nothing left for me here

No comfort, no hope

Since death won't visit me at will

I will visit death myself

I want to die by my arms

Because my life is in my hand.

I've lived long enough

If you will cry when I die

Start crying now

It doesn't bother me
I have become God
Nothing bothers Him.
My time is ripe.

Tell Dieye I am lost
Having lost every war I fought
Having been the topic of mockery
You think it hurts, well it doesn't hurt
I am numb from despair
Not that it matters anyway.

A man's heart is his home
On a dying house, I bloom
Because I'm a mushroom
Darkness surrounds my dome.

I can't be loved in this place
I've gone here and there.
I've looked in people's face
But there's no acceptance here.

Tell the world I search for peace
But I'm walking back
To the cities I dropped roses
But got a vase of tragedy

I'll etch my grief

On the sands of time

Thus, any child born

Will learn of my despair.

Tell Dieye I lost my empathy

There is no love in my eyes

But don't try to help me

I am a stagnant river

I can still drown people

Don't try to save my soul

I live to cause travails.

Ebom Tobe Churchill

Glimmer of Hope

Her silent ponderings filled the air
Like fog that would not lift
The loss of her beloved suddenly
Breaking anchor setting her adrift
Her heart ached with longing
As her whole world was tossed
Surges of emotional torment
Punctuating planned future now lost.

How could things change so quickly?
He had always been for her a rock
Without him what would she do
Amidst the grief, pain and shock?
No glimmer for days, weeks, months
Then as dawn broke there came light
Hope could just be seen ahead
Far off, but still within her sight.

Kate Brumby

◆ ◆ ◆

"When I think of flowers
Freckled in dew
I remember you
You are not the flower
You are the dew"

-Ebom Tobe Churchill-

◆ ◆ ◆

When the Sun Shines

When the sun shines
I'll write about my lover
Scribbling every line
With a smile.

When the rainbow comes
I'll buy her a rose
And watch her sniff the fragrance
I'll protect her.

When the rain stops
I'll take a walk with my lover
We will have a picnic
And I'll peek at her nipple
When no one watches.

When the dew dries

We will walk the bush path

I'll not let her cry

Because tears are for me

I'll lie to her that the world

Will never end.

But I have lost hope

That the rain will stop

I've forgotten the sun's warmth

What colors have the rainbow?

The dew rules the clime

And our world ends every day.

Ebom Tobe Churchill

Moon Lee

Following you
Has seen me blind
Hold my hand
Not to fall
Lead my feet
Away from the wall
And answer me, moon
Whenever I call
For the night is dark
Shivering with fear
Following you
Has seen me blind
Be on the lead
I'll follow behind
Be my shield
In this firing field
And be my host
Whenever I'm lost
For the night is dark
Shivering with fear.

Brian Ngusale

Suicide and Madness

Carry out no autopsy

I died of substance overdose

Or maybe suicide

My stomach is a pharmacy

Of heroin and other pills

My lungs no longer believe

In the existence of cancer

Because I should be a patient

But I'm not!

I want to see the look on God's face

When I sneeze out the life He gave

I have broken the bridges

God knows I won't look back

Let me burn in the fire

Then wallow in the frying pan

Where I die slowly.

If you see someone that loves me

Censor my biography

Or at least warn the readers

So they don't emulate me.

My mind is a haunted house

119

My language is on death row

I'm not addicted, I'm home

I'm trying to see the world

In a different picture

This war is needed

To find me peace.

I'll be dead before you know it

My pain will live on as guilt

In the heart of God

If He has the decency to own it.

Keep my story away

From children who think

The world is a garden

Leave people to their delusions

It is safer sometimes.

Maybe I should dive in an ocean

And make my plumage

As cold as my heart?

Then I'll fly across the world

And drop an ice on roofs

Below my frosty wings.

If you think it doesn't snow
In West Africa
I dare you to look into my heart
Look too hard, get frozen.

A mad man has picked up a pen
You just bought a book
Whose content is my despair
Well, I'm long dead and gone.

Ebom Tobe Churchill

Blue Life

I have tested the pills
I have drunk forbidden drinks
I've shot up dope
And smoked crank.

Living for the moment
The moment to be high
With drugs in my veins
I feel so alive.

Chasing that high
Day in and day out
Looking for *Oxycontin*
Never having any doubts.

My fears subsided
The quantities rose
Stealing from those
Who loved me most.

Pushing people away
I forgot how to care;
The looks on their faces
Not fazing me
At least not then or there.

Pushing the limits
Too many times;
Frozen in space
As it consumes my mind.

Nothing else matter
Not one bit;
Getting high is the life
And I will live it.

It was just a matter of time
Fun became memories
Stuck on rewind
Now I'm locked up
And stuck in my mind.

As I sit here, I feel I must say
I don't want to be here
For one more day.

Sentenced to six months
Behind the bricks
Chain linked fence
And barbed wire.

Made a mistake
That can't be erased;
Kicked down that door

I'm such a disgrace.

No one to turn to
Nor depend on;
The nights are cold
Days are long.

They just drag on
And on and on
Waiting to start again
Maybe I'll live great.

Hopes to be forgiven
Praying to a God
That is non-existent.

I walk the laps
Round and round
Going nowhere fast.

Replaying the horrid stories
Of my past regret
The clouds of time
Have changed my mind
About this life I can't rewind.

Take it all back
That is what I'd like to do

Knowing this can't be done
I cry boo-hoo.

I will accept my uncharted fate
Through countless mistakes
I continue to make
As lessons learned
To live by till my dying day.

Venessa Valdez

Seasons

Let us enjoy the seasons

And not complain too much

Of rains, heat and snow

Each has a role

In life's scheme

Surely, they will not

Last for ever

Seasons will change for sure

As sun sets or rises

Let us enjoy each season

With its blessings and curses

They teach us

Many lessons

Of patience, struggle

Tolerance and harvest

Let us welcome every season

With open arms

Seasons make us optimistic and philosophical.

Surendra Sahu

University Student

I see your confidence

You are talkative yet

Not too assuming

Yet not too shy and timid

Your socialization sounds healthy

Not exterior nor concentrated in character

Who are you really?

You have a love life

Yet you are serious in your studies

You are new and quiet

Yet you have a close relationship with your classmates

You are broke

Yet you have catchy and elegant clothes

You are hungry not full

You attend and participate in class

Should I call you a survivor?

Pass or fail

Your smile is still good and natural

You are an adult

Yet you are a student.

You are a student

You keep going at all costs

You do your assignments

You understand or not

You study always

You are fresh and healthy

Yet you have no food

You are a survivor.

Simphiwe Sihawu Dlamini

Broken Wings

His radiance was beautiful
As he soared above and beyond
Then life changed so suddenly
As with injury, hope was gone.

His broken spirit and body there
Cried out in surrendering pain
And within himself knew at once
He would never fly ever again.

She tried to comfort and sooth
To reassure and to him console,
But no words or any actions
Could bring healing to make him whole.

His wings and his heart shattered
All joy and reason were now lost
One moment of irresponsibility
Was being paid at full cost.

Disarmed, humiliated he lingered
She held him close and cried,
Telling him of her love so deep
He wept too and then sighed.

Together they may be stronger
Perhaps enough to again raise up,
As like the wings of eagles
Lifted in their and God's love.

Kate Brumby

Light-up Your Jaw

I love the way you laugh
I don't say it out these days
Your face depicts that times are rough
I hardly see the smiles on your face
Maybe there's no reason to smile.

Beauty went bankrupt on your face
Your skin is soft like a bird's newborn
And the smoothness mocks river stones
There seems to be diamond in your eye
Or the sun on its brightest gem
And coral lies in place of your bones
Yet I didn't love you enough.

Should I talk about your laugh
Which feels like good tiding?
Or tell you a story about your heart
Which defies gold in value?
The world would curse me
If I showed them your grace
Because I took you for granted.

I may withhold it when we see
That I love your beautiful smiles
These days you sit and look at me
Dragging your mistakes from miles
And every point of your memory.

And it hurts to think I'm your flaw
Who knows, until I hear your story
Whichever way, light up your jaw
With your beautiful smile
And forget about me.

Ebom Tobe Churchill

For Rosemary Edo-Osayi

Reality

I always get these thoughts inside my head
That make me think I would be better off dead
I sit in contemplation as the hours tick by
Thinking of the things that I should have done.

I distance myself from the world that surrounds me
But I still cannot escape this so-called reality
Neither am I able to determine the difference between
What is the truth and what is a lie.

I'm a science project sitting on the back shelf
Of something greater and bigger than I
People tell me I am crazy
My thoughts are insane.

Nobody understands my anguish, my pain
It's as though I'm not even real
Just matter vibrating in thin air
Yet this is my reality, not that you even care.

Venessa Valdez

He No Longer

He no longer feared her eyes
Even when she looked so nice
He no longer feared her eyes.

He no longer feared her voice
Even when she whispered so close
He no longer feared her voice.

He no longer saw her as an angel
Even when she bounced like a turkey
He no longer saw her as an angel.

He no longer saw her innocence
Even when she behaved like silence
He no longer saw her innocence.

Brian Ngusale

Loss

It wasn't so much the smile he gave
As the glint within his eyes
That told her of his deep love
And how his heart endlessly sighed.

It wasn't so much the touch he gave
As the feeling that brewed and surged
That told her of his longing
And of how he ached for only her.

It wasn't so much what he said
As the silence they together shared
It had told her of his understanding
And how he unreservedly cared.

His smile, his touch, his calm repose
These were what struck her mind
As she knew one hundred percent
Another like him she'd not find.

Being asked to marry was inevitable
The two fitting together perfectly
Then as weeks turned to months
In union they soon became three.

A child bonded them even closer
She made a beautiful home and mum
They felt complete and blessed
To them heaven on earth had come.

Then things changed tragically
She and son killed while traveling
He had no idea what to do next
How a new life alone to begin.

He searched for a quick console
And found it within a bottle red
But all drinking did was temporary
Only his sadness and guilt was fed.

He wrestled daily with emotion
His feelings overtook his life
No longer able to live in the present
He wanted his past, his son, his wife.

Days then weeks rolled into months
Year on year moved on but not him
Stuck as though time stood still
Until suddenly he felt bizarrely nothing.

He had no idea what had happened
There was no cause just an effect
As in the beating of his own heart
He could be on his own future set.

He resolved to help others from then on
To support them in grief and loss
In doing so his wife would live on
As in this she'd be helping him focus.

Kate Brumby

◆ ◆ ◆

"I'm tempted to hang out with them
Who left thinking
pen is my only chum
I've stopped sharing my feelings
Diary is the place they like
their dwelling"

-Simran Munot-

◆ ◆ ◆

Hidden

You see a smile on the outside

But that's all you can see

What if tears run down my face on the inside?

You hear a laugh on the outside

But that's all you can hear

What if I'm crying out for help on the inside?

You smell the scent I wear every day on the outside

But that's all you can smell

What if it smells of death on the inside?

You feel soft, smooth skin on the outside

But that's all you feel

What if I'm being torn apart on the inside?

You taste sweet lips kissing you on the outside

But that's all you can taste

What if my lips taste of blood on the inside?

You can tell I'm happy on the outside

But what if you can't tell I'm dying on the inside?

Simphiwe Sihawu Dlamini

I Said This on a Platter of Tears

Dearly beloved

Fate has led me astray

I douse myself in alcohol

Everyday

Hoping to bath clean

But I won't stop reeking

Of defeat.

I have some powder

Hidden somewhere in my car

It only takes a sniff or two

To forget the stories of my scar

But just for a moment.

Well just for the records

I can only pass a drug test

If I took it from a flying pig

My stomach is made of pills.

I hardly sleep in my bed

I'm always shaking like I have flu

At the dark corners of my room

My eyes are pale, the colors red

Yet my world still remains blue.

Put on your dress, woman!
The waters of your vagina
Cannot wash my grief away
Well, nothing can anyway
I'm not the man for you
My whole life is rumpled
I've never found peace
And I'm tired to pretend
It doesn't bother me.

My lines will start its tour
Before I shoot myself
Maybe some will miss me
As Kate Brumby misses Stu
Not like I care so much.

There's drainage in my soul
My spirit flow away
My legs have touched places
Where nothing but anguish festered
My heart is coal, my heart is snow
My feelings have gone astray
My eye can boil the North Pole
For it makes volcano feel cold.

The sun shines everyday
Yet I'm still alone
Why take the blade away?

So I don't cut my wrist

Why don't you take me?

Why don't we go away

To a place of bliss?

No one is coming for me;

I'm a cobweb bred in isolation;

My arm has become to my shin;

A velvet of consolation

But I'm doing good

With my pills.

I want to go to sleep

Tell my people!

Or anyone that cares to know

It's my life after all

Even though I couldn't find its meaning

I couldn't find a reason

To live in this cursed world.

Morning to evening, tears!

I'm not doing this again

Here I stand empty

Falling side by side the path

Like a madman.

I'll give you no further burden

Just open up the earth

Throw me in, I'm done!
When you pass by my resting nest
Know beneath is a madman
That tried his best
To make a meaning out of the world.

My spirit is long dead
My frame is following suit
My heart is always scared
At the dawn of a new day
Gbim gbim gbim gbim
It's always beating so fast
And beating so heavy
As if in a haste to discharge
The whole breath of what's left
In my pathetic life
In just one day.

We are all born free
But we must die as slaves
To this wanton life
The world is meaningless
So is our existence
And there's nothing we can do
About it.

I may have a chance in my next life
Mtcheew there's no next life

We can only boast of now
Sorry, we can't boast of nothing
Just lay me down to rest.

There's no grudge in my heart
I'm going to sleep
This time with a sedative
And if I will wake up
I should wake up as dust.

I want to lay beside Ndidi
Oh, precious Ndidi
The sunrise and sunset
Of my thoughts.

When I die soon
Tell the world I was unfortunate
Tell them I cried everyday
And I lived my life in hate
When people smile
Let them know I tried too
Even when I wanted to die
Tell them I was cold like dew.

Ebom Tobe Churchhill

I am Writing with Vengeance

Reluctantly I stopped to flaunt
For, I couldn't take continuous taunts
They say *Instagram* means pictures
But not write-ups with your signatures
I decided to put my pen down
For a confession wrenched me deep down.

Thoughts of my comrades left me forked
They said they were irked
I stopped writing, for it left me isolated
Never realized the long differences it created.
Feels like I'm a soul boycotted by all
Confined in chamber concreted walls
I stopped writing for I'm also a human
I crave for real friends but not illusion.

I'm tempted to hang out with them
Who left thinking pen is my only chum
I've stopped sharing my feelings
Diary is the place they like their dwelling.
She's the real companion unlike beings
Understands me though she has no feelings.

Simran Munot

Konchella

If I am to sublime

In this well of lime

Let me like etherized iodine

To the air where I'll be hidden.

If it's this ridge of age

Seeking to seal our page

Let's wait then until

Our hearts open at will.

If it's our outlying race

That will set up a civil case

Let me carry my in-laws` curio arm

Until those judgments are per-in-curium.

If it's my silence

That will amount not to acceptance

Then let me cross the distance

To your village and carry a spear.

Give me those skins to wear

And let's hear if they will sphere

Their words up to here

If I am to sublime.

Brian Ngusale

What Am I?

A farmer said *I'd be rainy*
If I was a season, and a lime
If I was a fruit, and a vulture
If I could fly,
I nodded.

.

An ostrich called me her egg.
Why then are you left in the dust?
With reckless abandon
Forgotten to be trodden.
Still, I nodded.

.

A hawk mocked, *you are a chick*
In a blink, your life is gone.
A mourner swore I was sadder
And queried why my dress
Is always black
I nodded.

The ant called me their hill.
What have you done despite the hollows.
Running through your heart?
I nodded.

A man in death row spoke his mind

You are already a ghost

Your life is in my spit,

I nodded.

A historian searching for peace

Mourned the war in my soul

You are the first born of Egyptians

In the reign of Pharaoh.

A beggar with an empty plate

Sneered in my path

My belly is empty,

So is your soul!

And he put his money on it.

What in God's name are you?!

Asked an armadillo

That has no past.

Ebom Tobe Churchill

Bury Me Here

Bury me here not by the Sea
In this escaping beauty where I see
Bury me here incase I'll die
I beseech you now and don't ask why.

Bury me here when I'll fly
Out of this life oh! I'm shy
Bury me here when I'll be null
Like an infinite upon my fall.

Bury me here although I'm bad
Remember all chronicles I am only a lad
Bury me here in this sinking soil
To let me disperse and since don't toil.

Bury me here where I desire
Never let me go it's not a satire
Bury me here in a wooden casket
And like tears of trial let me cascade.

Bury me here not in a golden cup
Of high admiralties but let me be hope
Bury me here in this drumming despair
Of this sainting somewhere to let me de-pair.

Bury me here where I feel free
Like a harvested soul near a tall tree
Bury me here in this half like liquor
When I'll say goodbye to my mother Africa.

Brian Ngusale

Hourglass

The room is empty.

I knock to walk into the emptiness,

Listening to the thousand decibels of silence,

And casting my mind back.

Till the sand is on the other side one last time.

Collecting all the memories we scattered around the room,

Hearing every sweet word of forever

I feel the love we had,

I feel the adjuring that went in vain.

Letting go the sand would be easier.

I could remember everything,

I could feel everything

The sound of me when I cried,

Your screams that pierced into my ears.

Time's up.

It's hard to imagine sand at the bottom,

Because this moment won't last forever.

But - That is what makes it special.

Simran Munot

My Soldier Boy (a dirge)

The sun's troubles are now over
No more noise from guns and cries,
Or more gores to make you shiver
My soldier boy now, rest your eyes.

Your finger's free from trigger's greed
Your feet won't cow'r to fields of mines,
Neith'r shall you fall again and bleed
My soldier boy, how life declines.

You need no clouds, my eyes make rain
And my rain won't stop while you sleep,
Although no pains live in your brain
My soldier boy, you make me weep.

When I lay you in your cold room
Inside earth's womb, where mortals fear,
You don't have to dread any gloom
My soldier boy, no dream is there.

Just so soon, you befriend the night?
Well, sleep, dear, sleep, all heroes must
Forget your guns; there's no more fight
My soldier boy, you don't fight in dust.

Your war is ov'r, 'tis time to rest
Let those awake filter the grain
F'get the ranks on your shoulder's vest
You cannot suffer loss or gain!

Everyone says goodbye someday
Goodbyes are sadd'r when time is brief,
You should've stay'd for one more day
My soldier boy, I sing in grief.

Your fight and fear, and creed is gone
So is the sun, I'm covered in dew,
But what can I do since you are done?
My soldier boy, goodbye to you.

Ebom Tobe Churchill

About the Authors

Kate Brumby

Kate is a self-published British Poet who writes a mixture of Christian, anecdotal and humorous rhyming verse. Kate's debut poetry collection *In the Palm of His Hand* ©2019 has proven to be popular as a book for personal devotion. Kate's memoir, *His Guiding Hand* ©2020 interweaves over 120 poems with narrative to provide an inspiring account of her life.

Kate and her husband share their home with a dog, Dottie- her name chosen as it means 'gift of God'. In addition to writing, Kate enjoys church related activities and a diverse range of hobbies including arts and crafts, singing, playing several musical instruments, gardening, and walking.

Kate is always happy to be contacted by readers via her website
www.katebrumby.co.uk

Or by social media:
Facebook @PoetBrumby
Instagram @Kate_Brumby_Poet_Author
Twitter @PoetBrumby

Ebom Tobe Churchill

Ebom Tobe Churchill is a Nigerian poet and storyteller. He describes his existence as unnecessary, and as a huge tragedy. So much despair is often expressed in his works. Watching Ndidi die after a crash has planted a timeless grief in his heart. Ndidi was 47.

He loves nothing. He worships nothing. He wishes to publish most of his written works and die at a very young age.

Facebook Ebom Tobe Churchill
Twitter @ebomTobe
Instagram @ebomtobechurchill

Simphiwe Sihawu Dlamini

Born in Manzini, Swaziland on July 30, 1999, Simphiwe grew up in a small township called KaKhoza, Manzini. The township was categorized by a high crime rate and at the tender age of 3, he lost his father due to an accident. From the point on he was raised by his widowed mother and his two brothers of which his is the youngest.

As a small boy Simphiwe had big dreams, focused well in school and in 2017 he graduated from high school. From that point on he began to write poetry professionally; his love and passion growing tremendously. Online poetry courses kept him busy while awaiting his tertiary education enrolment to be accepted.

Facebook Sihawu Dlamini
Twitter @sihawuDlamini
Instagram SihawuDK

Simran Munot

Simran loves switching on light bulbs with people- facilitating those 'aha moments' that change mindsets and open new possibilities. Sorted in Gryffindor, she is an avid reader and a big foodie. She is one of those women code with a demonstrated history working in the creative design and development industry. You better don't go on her age. For her age is just a number. Being an entrepreneur is supposed to be in her blood. Co-Founder of Lapsus Next and Lapsus Creations, she leads the company with a lot of enthusiasm and discipline.

Writing is her passion as she writes what she feels and observes in society. She is a city-dweller who loves to travel, meet new people, develop new relationships, solve problems in a creative way and find new adventures along the way. You can find her in front of her laptop if not eating or reading. You can connect with her anytime on any social media. Just type in her full name and boom you will find her because her name is as unique as she is!

Facebook Simran Munot
Twitter @SimranMunot
Instagram @simran.penwomen
LinkedIn Simran Munot

Brian Ngusale

Brian is a Kenyan born writer, poet, accountant, practicing barista and the first born in a family of five. He is an avid reader and has a great passion for learning. He is the author of *Where the Light Leads* and looks forward to publishing three more books in 2020, including a devotional.

He has been a student of poetry and writing for more than ten years. Brian is a passionate reader of great books. Aside from reading, he enjoys listening to music and praying. Currently living in Nairobi where he looks forward to starting a family with his beautiful girlfriend.

Twitter @Bngusale
Instagram @brian_ngusale

Surendra Sahu

Born in Odisha, India in 1950, Surendra is an engineer and manager by profession. He has been writing poetry since the age of thirteen. His first collection *Trapped Animal* was published by Writers Workshop in 1989. Since then he has published some seventy odd books on Amazon KDP since 2012.

His best-selling book *similes and metaphors* has sold over 1000 copies worldwide. He writes on management topics and self-help. He has translated some titles from Hindi and Odia into English. Currently living in Hyderabad, India with is family, spending his days gardening, reading, and travelling after retirement from the government in 2010.

Facebook Surendra.k.sahu
Instagram @sksahu06

Venessa Valdez

Venessa was raised by her loving dad who still is her everything in the small town of Placerville in northern California. Her teenage years were filled with poor choices that led to a seemingly endless misery where writing was the only outlet, she uses her traumatic experiences to bring comfort to those who can relate. She has been beaten, raped, addicted to drugs and abused mentally and physically by those she once called friends.

Helping others through trials in their lives is her greatest passion. She has assisted with organizing food and toy drives by preparing flyers and writing appreciation letters to supporters. A high school graduate who appreciates the art and beauty of poetry.

Writer of *Lost Friendships,* a poem that received The Editor's Choice Award for displaying a unique perspective and original creativity from the International Library of Poetry. She never goes anywhere without a pad of paper and a pen because the words are in her soul and meant to be shared.

Facebook Venessa Christine Valdez
Instagram @valdezvenessa

GLOSSARY

Abweido-

An African name. A stream in Ubulu-Unor. Ubulu-Unor is a village in Nigeria. Ebom Tobe Churchill is a native of the village.

Benue-

A river located in Africa, specifically in Nigeria. It meets with the river Niger, and both are represented as the letter Y in the Nigerian Coat of Arm.

Day of Silence-

This is an event that happened on January 1, 2008 in Rift Valley Kenya during the Post-election violence.

Edumeku-

The grandmother of Author and poet Ebom Tobe Churchill. She is the mother of Ndidi.

Harmattan-

A very cold season in Nigeria known for dry breezes that cause very dry skin.

Hiawatha-

Child of Wenonah and the West-Wind from the book *The Song of Hiawatha,* by Henry Wordsworth Longfellow.

Holi-

An Indian festival where people throw or sprinkle colors on each other.

Job-

A biblical character that suffered great woes even though he was upright.

Kofi Awoonor-

A Ghanaian poet, well known for his poem *Songs of Sorrows.* Much of his work used symbolism to depict Africa during decolonization.

Kylie Jenner-

Stars in TV series Keeping Up with the Kardashians since 2007 and is the owner and founder of Kylie Cosmetics.

Limpopo-

A river in South Africa that flows to the Indian Ocean.

Lot's wife-

>This is the wife of the biblical character, Lot. She turned to a pillar of salt after looking back at Sodom. Known in some Jewish tradition as Edith or Ado, though she is unnamed in the Bible.

Mtcheew-

>A hissing sound, commonly made by Nigerians that show dissatisfaction,   annoyance, disapproval, malice…

Ndidi-

>The mother of poet Ebom Tobe Churchill.

Nne-

>'Mother' in African language. Commonly used when addressing a lady.

River Kiang-

>An ancient Chinese reference to a section of River Yangtze, the longest river in Asia and third longest river in the world.

Tempora Munantur-

>A Latin adage that refers to the changes that the passage of time brings. It appears in   various longer hexametric forms, most commonly Tempora Munantur, nos et mutamur in illis which translate in English to Times are changed, we also are changed with them.

Walls of Jericho-

>Mentioned in the Bible. It was told that soldiers danced round the walls seven times while they sang praise to God, and the walls collapsed, while they won the fight against Jericho.

Yolanda/ Yolani-

>Yolani was intended to mean happiness as it was used in the poem where her absence is mourned.

Zambezi-

>The fourth longest river in Africa, the longest east-flowing river in Africa,   and the largest flowing into the Indian Ocean from

Africa.